MW00469211

FEARLESS

FEARLESS
Living Life the Way God Intended

Chad Gonzales

Auxano Publications

FEARLESS-
Living Life the Way God Intended
ISBN-13: 978-0-9777380-0-7
ISBN-10: 0-9777380-0-0
Library of Congress Control Number: 2006900278

Copyright © 2006,2014 Chad W. Gonzales
www.chadgonzales.com

Published by Auxano Publications   SAN 8 5 0 – 1 0 8 4

Table of Contents

1.   Melted Hearts   11

2.   The Result of Knowledge   31

3.   The Answer for Fear   37

4.   The Identity of Fear   49

5.   Knock, Knock   59

6.   Mind Control   67

7.   Continual Awareness   87

     STUDY GUIDE   95

Preface

Would you consider yourself fearful or fearless? After taking an honest look at one's thoughts, words, and actions, the large majority of Christians would probably choose fearful. For too long, we as Christians have walked through life intimidated, worried, stressed and downright scared; this should not be the case.

Have you ever noticed how many Christians live life timidly? It would be impossible to count the number of times I have heard people say, "I am afraid of this" or "That scares me."

Honestly, I can remember plenty of times when I made those statements; yet, every time those words came out of my mouth, I would get a check in my spirit. As I grew up spiritually, I learned that was the Holy Spirit trying to teach me.

You see, the Holy Spirit is our teacher and we must look to Him for direction in our life. Sometimes, He may speak to you by way of a vision, dream or an audible voice; but, the vast majority of time, it will be a simple "nudge." Some have described it as a check or a scratch on the inside, while others have compared it to a red or green light.

Colossians 3:15 tells us to let the peace of God rule in our hearts. We are to always follow peace; if there is no peace regarding a situation or a decision, stop what you are doing and see what the Holy Spirit is trying to show you. But always, always respond immediately to His words, because if you continue to ignore His leading, you will harden your heart in that area. If your heart has become calloused, it will be difficult to hear from Him; therefore, we must endeavor to always be sensitive to His voice and then immediately obey.

For me it took a few "nudgings," because I can be quite stubborn at times, but I finally realized that those fear statements should never come out of a Christian's mouth. "Fear," as well as "poor" and "sick" are no different than any other nasty four-letter word. They are filth from our mouth. Why? We are speaking against God's Word. We are saying that we are opposite of what God made us to be. God made us to be healthy, wealthy and confident!

We are to be people of faith, not people of fear; besides, living by fear is a sin. Did you ever stop to think about that? Every time you get in fear, you are in sin. I am certainly not trying to condemn you, but simply make you aware of it. The Bible says that anything that is not of faith is sin. Well, fear is definitely not faith; therefore we must get rid of fear in our lives and start living by faith. The faith life is what we were created to live and it is the faith life we must determine to live.

Our Heavenly Father designed us to be fearless and live as bold as a lion. Think about the attitude of a lion. Have you ever seen a lion running away from another animal? No, they are always the hunter running after the hunted. They are the rulers of the jungle; they are the giants in the land. Physically, there may be other animals larger in size, but the lion does not know that and neither do the others. The lion is king and is always the *intimidator* not the *intimidated!*

We have dealt with fear in this way and that way, but never in the right way. If we want Bible results, then we must follow Bible directions. There is a Bible way to dealing with each and every situation; fear is not an exception.

My aim is to equip you with the Bible knowledge you need to have Bible results; thus, giving you the opportunity to obliterate fear in your life. My purpose in this writing is to simply lay out the Word of God concerning the subject of fear and allow the Word to simply speak for itself.

I pray you will have complete comprehension and understanding and that wisdom and revelation will come in light of what you read. Allow the Holy Spirit to teach you, lead you and guide you throughout this study. He will lead you in all things as He will in this book. Praise God for His goodness!

Fearful or fearless? I choose fearless!

Chapter One

Melted Hearts

On March 4, 1932, President Franklin D. Roosevelt gave one of the most memorable inaugural addresses in history. Within the first moments of his speech, President Roosevelt made the following statement:

> "...let me assert my firm belief that the only thing we have to fear is fear itself- nameless, unreasoning, unjustified terror which paralyzes needed efforts to convert retreat into advance."

In the midst of the Great Depression, President Roosevelt understood the feelings and thoughts of the American people; he also understood that in order for America to go forward, the fear of the nation had to be removed.

Friends, fear will keep you from prospering in life. It will hinder you spiritually, physically, mentally, socially, and financially; it will stop growth in every area of your existence. In order for you to go forward in life, your life must be dominated by faith, not dominated by fear. In short, the results of fear unhindered will destroy you.

In the book of Joshua, we can clearly see the effects of fear in one's life. After the death of Moses, Joshua sent two men to spy out the land which God had given Israel. While in Jericho, Rahab the harlot made the following statements to the spies:

> I know that the Lord has given you the land, that the terror of you has fallen on us, and that all the inhabitants of the land are fainthearted because of you. For we have heard how the Lord dried up the water of the Red Sea for you when you came out of Egypt, and what you did to the two kings of the Amorites who were on the other side of the Jordan, Sihon and Og, whom you utterly destroyed. And as soon as we heard these things, our hearts melted; neither did there remain any more courage in anyone because of you, for the Lord your God, He is God in heaven above and on earth beneath.
>
> Joshua 2:9-11

After hearing what God had done for Israel, Rahab said the inhabitants of the land were terrified. Did you notice how fear affected them? Their hearts melted!

> And as soon as we heard these things, our hearts melted; neither did there remain any courage in anyone...
>
> Joshua 2:11

Now of course their literal hearts were not melted; this phrase meant their hope, courage and strength was destroyed. The will of the people was demolished. Fear had totally taken away all hope for victory against the Israelites. You see, fear softens; faith hardens. Fear weakens you; faith strengthens you.

In Joshua 5:1, we find similar statements regarding Israel and their enemies.

So it was, when all the kings of the Amorites who were on the west side of the Jordan, and all the kings of the Canaanites who were by the sea, heard that the Lord had dried up the waters of the Jordan from before the children of Israel until we had crossed over, that their hearts melted; and there was no spirit in them any longer because of the children of Israel.

Again, we see the results of fear: melted hearts. When the kings of the Amorites and Canaanites heard what God had done for Israel, their hearts melted. Fear had dissolved their will to win. They knew that defeat was imminent; the Bible says they had no spirit left. In other words, all hope, all courage and all strength had departed.

You see, to live the life of faith, their must be hope. Hebrews 11:1 says, "Now faith is the substance of things hoped for..." *The strength of your faith in God's Word will be no greater than your expectation that God's Word will come to pass.* If you want results, there must be an expectancy that God's Word will come to pass in your life!

There is a vast difference between the natural hope of the world and the Bible hope of God. Natural hope is wishing something will come to pass; another words, it is full of doubt. In contrast, Bible hope is an assured expectation that God's Word will come to pass! Hope is necessary to obtain the promises of God and live a victorious life.

Just as fear robbed the Amorites and Canaanites, fear will rob you of your hope. It will take away your "want to"- your want to win. Fear will melt your heart and destroy any hope of winning the battle you are facing. With a melted heart, you would not have the strength or the ability to press onward.

Ultimately, fear destroys you and nullifies the life, abilities and anointing which you possess. Regardless of what talents God has given you or the level of anointing He has placed upon you, fear will put a sudden and severe halt on them...if you allow fear in your life. Why? It requires faith to use what God has given you. Faith and fear are not best friends; they are enemies and can not coexist in your heart.

A third instance of melted hearts is found in Joshua 7:1, 5.

> **But the children of Israel committed a trespass regarding the accursed things for Achan the son of Carmi, the son of Zabdi, the son of Zerah, of the tribe of Judah, took of the accursed things; so the anger of the LORD burned against the children of Israel. And the men of Ai struck down about thirty-six men, for they chased them from before the gate as far as Shebarim, and struck them down on the descent; therefore the hearts of the people melted and became like water.**

In this situation, it was the children of Israel whose hearts melted. Why did their hearts melt? The Israelites had sinned against God and as a result, God was no longer fighting for them. Israel's enemy had defeated them and the children of Israel were terrified. They had lost their hope, courage and strength in regards to defeating the enemy.

A melted heart produces a weak man; a melted heart produces a coward. Show me someone who is weak, scared, or terrified and I will show you someone with a melted heart. If you haven't understood it yet, understand it now...fear melts hearts! Isaiah even prophesied that people's hearts will melt from fear during the tribulation.

> **Wait, for the day of the LORD is at hand! It will come as destruction from the Almighty. Therefore all hands will be limp. Every man's heart will melt, And they will be afraid.**
>
> **Isaiah 13:6, 7**

Something I find very interesting within Joshua 7:5 is the comparison of the heart melting like water. It doesn't say their hearts melted a little bit or even became somewhat soggy; it states their hearts became as water. It brings to mind that of an ice cube. If you were to place an ice cube outside in the Texas heat, it would not take much time for the ice cube to turn into water; given enough exposure to the heat, the water will evaporate. In the same respect, if you place your heart under the influence of fear, it will not only melt, but could eventually fade away.

The point I am trying to make is this: the longer fear has an influence, the more your heart will melt, until you have absolutely no hope, no courage, and no strength. Fear is not something to take lightly; it will burn you and with enough time, it will take you out of the picture completely. The longer you allow fear to stay in your life, the more of a stronghold it will have over your life.

One summer, I was helping at a kid's camp and they were participating in an extreme obstacle course. One of the obstacles consisted of climbing a 30 foot telephone pole. Once they were standing atop the pole,   they had to jump approximately 5 feet and grab hold of a trapeze bar. Now of course, they were totally safe. Each child was wearing a safety harness and danger was not an issue…but fear definitely was.

One girl climbed the pole and was in position to jump. She yelled "One, two, three!" and did not move an inch. So the camp instructor down below counted with her. Again, "One, two, three!" yet she didn't budge. When the instructor asked what was wrong, the young girl responded, "I can't get my legs to move!" We on the ground thought it was really funny, but the young girl wasn't laughing! The problem was she wanted to complete the obstacle, but she was so scared, she couldn't move forward. Fear had melted her heart.

After about 15 minutes, she had given up and tried to climb down; yet, she didn't realize that in the way the obstacle was designed, there was no way down except to jump! After a few more minutes of encouragement from below, she finally jumped. She missed the trapeze bar, but laughed the whole time she was being lowered down.

Fear had taken away her expectation she would grab the trapeze bar; fear had taken away her confidence that she could complete the task; fear had taken away her strength to physically move.

I can remember times growing up when I was so scared, I couldn't move. I would physically try to run away or scream for help, yet I could not do anything; it simply paralyzed me. We have all been in those situations and we see it portrayed in media. People become so scared they are stopped cold in their tracks; their hearts melt and they become a victim of fear.

My last example of melted hearts is found in Joshua 14:6-8.

> **The children of Judah came to Joshua in Gilgal. And Caleb the son of Jephunneh the Kenizzite said to him: "You know the word which the LORD said to Moses the man of God concerning you and me in Kadesh Barnea. I was forty years old when Moses the servant of the LORD sent me from Kadesh Barnea to spy out the land and I brought back word to him as it was in my heart. Nevertheless my brethren who went up with me made the heart of the people melt, but I wholly followed the LORD my God."**

Because of the evil report, the hearts of Israel melted. Their melted hearts caused them to lose all hope, all courage, and all strength; consequently, they abandoned the promise that God had given to them. Yet, notice Caleb's last statement: *"...but I wholly followed the LORD my God."* Caleb rejected fear, held fast to his faith and held on to God's Word. As a result, Caleb received the inheritance God promised.

GOD REQUIRES FAITH

You may have never thought about it, but fear is just as powerful as faith. Fear will keep you *from acting* on God's Word just as much as faith will *keep you acting* on God's Word.

How many of us have had instances in our lives when God was telling us to do something and we honestly wanted to obey, but were simply too scared to do so. He had given you the instructions, assured your safety, given you the ability, and supplied all the equipment; yet, you didn't complete the task because you were scared. Despite all that He had done and provided, you looked to your situation and your feelings instead of your God and your faith.

I am sure we can all relate in some way or another. We have all had experiences in which we stopped in our obedience because of fear. What about those times when you knew He was telling you to go witness to a particular person and you failed to do so because of possible rejection? I will be the first to admit I have been there and done that! Sadly, I let fear of rejection keep me from telling someone about Jesus.

Although, it is really absurd when you think about it, especially when you read the Bible! People are not rejecting you, they are rejecting Him. God's process and procedures are not to be of our concern, for we know the outcome is always success! The only concern we should have is, "Are we being obedient to God's Word?" If fear is dominating you, the answer to this question is an absolute "No."

IT MUST BE STOPPED

We have seen the danger of fear in that it will result in melted hearts; yet, I would like to break down the dangers of fear even further. I want you to see in a practical manner how it can affect our daily Christian walk. In searching the Word of God, I have found seven reasons why fear must be stopped in our lives.

Number one: Fear is contagious

Before Moses died, he gave a farewell speech to the Israelites. Within his speech, he gave the Israelites instructions regarding warfare. I would like to draw your attention to Deuteronomy 20:8.

> **The officers shall speak further to the people, and say, 'What man is there who is fearful and fainthearted? Let him go and return to his house, lest the heart of his brethren faint like his heart.'**

I don't know about you, but if I am going into battle, I do not want my fellow soldiers to be scared. Why? Fear is contagious; it spreads like a disease. I want to be surrounded by courage and hope, not fear and despair. In regards to faith, I need people around me who believe God's Word will come to pass. I do not want doubters around me because they will try to spread their unbelief.

This brings to mind a situation which occurred with my high school teammates. I remember one game in which we were to play the number one team in the state of Texas. During the pre-game warm-ups, I was excited because we were playing the best of the best and I craved the challenge. Even though the odds were against us, everyone on the team was confident except for one.

As we left the huddle to begin the game, this guy said, "I hope we don't get beat by more than 50." Every member of our team heard it, and slowly but surely, you could see despair begin to form on their faces. The longer they thought about it, the more their hearts melted. In ten seconds, fear spread and one melted heart turned into 12 melted hearts. From the tip-off, the opposing team threw an alley-oop from half court for a ferocious dunk; needless to say, it went downhill from that point.

Because of one person's fearful remark, almost the entire team went from expecting to compete to expecting an embarrassing defeat. After spending the entire first half trying to encourage my teammates, my coach and I finally got the team's spirit lifted, but it was too late. Even though a few of us believed we could win, we were outnumbered by fearful people; thus, we went home devastated losers.

Number two: Fear keeps you from
obtaining the promises of God

In Numbers 13, Moses and the Israelites were set to enter Canaan, the land God had promised them. Upon their arrival, Moses sent twelve spies to survey the land and bring back a report. Ten of the spies told the people about the giants in the land and how the Israelites would be crushed and defeated, never being able to possess the land. Consequently, the Israelites became fearful and doubted God's Word. Look at God's response to their fear and doubt:

> ...they certainly shall not see the land of which I swore to their fathers, nor shall any of those who rejected Me see it, but My servant Caleb. Because he has a different spirit in him and has followed Me fully,

I will bring into the land where he went, and his descendants shall inherit it.

Numbers 14:23, 24

As a consequence, they wandered in the desert for forty years until all those with melted hearts died. They allowed fear to overtake them and never obtained God's promise.

God has so many wonderful things simply waiting for you to grasp, but it will only be by faith that you obtain God's precious promises. Whether you realize it or not, God's promises are conditional. He always keeps His part, but it is your responsibility to act on His Word in faith. Regardless of what God has promised you in His Word, if you are operating in fear, you will never obtain it.

Number three: Fear keeps you from pleasing God

I don't know about you, but my greatest desire is to please my Heavenly Father. There is nothing in this world more important to me than pleasing my Father and fulfilling His desires and plans for my life.   Unless I live a life of faith, I will never begin to please Him.

But without faith it is impossible to please Him, for he who comes to God must believe that He is, and that He is a rewarder of those who diligently seek Him.

Hebrews 11:6

Faith is trust in God's Word; fear is doubt in God's Word. If you want to please God, it will only occur by living and walking by faith.

Faith is how God operates and it is how He expects you to operate.

**But he who doubts is condemned if he eats, because he does not eat
from faith; for whatever is not from faith is sin.**

Romans 14:23

Well, fear is obviously not faith, therefore it is sin. Fear is sin! We
know that sin does not please God; therefore, fear does not please
God. Remember, it is only by faith that we can please Him. Every
time we become fearful, we step out of the realm of faith.

Number four: Fear opens the door to Satan

We often wonder why things are going wrong in our lives. The vast
majority of time, it is because we have allowed Satan free reign in
our life. We open our mouths and confess the fear we are feeling
or thinking and immediately open the door to Satan. Now you may
think you have never done that, but honestly, we all have at some
point in our lives. You see, many Christians still do not have the
slightest understanding of the authority God has given us. We must
begin to implement the authority God has delegated to us! *You
control God's movement in your life just as much as you control
Satan's movement in your life.* You open the door to God with faith;
you open the door to Satan with fear. When you get into sin, you
step out of the umbrella of God's protection and open yourself up to
an unarmored attack by Satan.

A perfect example of this is found in the book of Job. Now we all
think about poor old Job as some guy in whom God just poured out

His wrath and tested like no other. "God was just mean to poor old Job" some have said. No, the truth of the matter was that Job was living in fear; consequently, God had to justly back off and allow certain things to happen. Let's look at Job 3:25, 26.

For the thing I greatly feared has come upon me, And what I dreaded has happened to me. I am not at ease, nor am I quiet; I have no rest, for trouble comes.

Job had been afraid of his children dying and losing his material possessions. He was living in fear and not in faith; thus, Satan had free reign to move in and God could not do anything about it. Yes, I repeat, God could do nothing about the situation because Job had a choice in the situation. Job's choice was fear, not faith. Just like Job, we have the choice of who we let into our lives. Live a life of obedience to God and you keep God in; live a life of sin and you unknowingly let Satan in and shove God out. Would you like a word of advice? Now brace your self because this is really deep! Here it is: Keep Satan out and keep God in!

Number five: Fear will cause you
to abandon your beliefs.

Do you know how strong fear is? Fear is so strong that it will cause you to divorce the truth. Something which you so strongly believe in, you could drop like a hot piece of coal if you become fearful. Would you like an example? Look at the life of Peter. Peter knew Jesus was the Christ; Peter believed Jesus was the Son of God. Peter walked with Jesus for over three years and trusted Him with his life, even vowing to die for Him.

> Now Peter sat outside in the courtyard. And a servant girl came to him, saying, "You also were with Jesus of Galilee." But he denied it before them all, saying, "I do not know what you are saying." And when he had gone out to the gateway, another girl saw him and said to those who were there, "This fellow also was with Jesus of Nazareth." But again he denied with an oath, "I do not know the Man!" And a little later those who stood by came up and said to Peter, "Surely you also are one of them, for your speech betrays you." Then he began to curse and swear, saying, "I do not know the Man!" Immediately a rooster crowed. And Peter remembered the word of Jesus who had said to him, "Before the rooster crows, you will deny Me three times." So he went out and wept bitterly.
>
> Matthew 25:69-75

Because of fear, Peter abandoned the Truth; not once, but three times in one setting. Fear caused Peter to let go of that in which he so fervently believed. If fear caused Peter to abandon the Word, then fear can cause you to abandon the Word.

How many times have you looked at your checkbook and wondered how you would get enough money for the rest of your bills? You become stressed and fearful that the lights might get cut off or the car repossessed, when all the while, you know God's promises of provision. Regardless of how much of a faith man or faith woman you think you are, if you allow fear into a certain area of your life, you will abandon God's Word in that area of your life.

Number six: Fear will keep you from
fulfilling God's plan for your life

In order for you to fulfill God's plan for your life, you will need two things: faith and obedience. Without these two items, you can kiss God's destiny for your life goodbye. Many times it will seem like you will have to give up your goals, desires and possibly some material possessions; but remember, God is a giver and not a taker. Whatever you turn over to Him will come back to you in a bountiful, abundant way. Faith will also be needed because whatever God has called you to do, you will not be able to accomplish in your own strength. Fulfilling your destiny will require faith in God; obedience will then be needed to put your faith into action.

A wonderful example of this is found in Matthew 19:16-22.

> Now behold, one came and said to Him, "Good Teacher, what good thing shall I do that I may have eternal life?" So He said to him, "Why do you call Me good? No one is good but One, that is, God. But if you want to enter into life, keep the commandments." He said to Him, "Which ones?" Jesus said, "'You shall not murder,' 'You shall not commit adultery,' 'You shall not steal,' 'You shall not bear false witness,' Honor your father and your mother,' and, 'You shall love your neighbor as yourself.' "The young man said to Him, "All these things I have kept from my youth. What do I still lack?" Jesus said to him, "If you want to be perfect, go, sell what you have and give to the poor, and you will have treasure in heaven; and come, follow Me." But when the young man heard that saying, he went away sorrowful, for he had great possessions.

You see, God's destiny for this young man was to be one of Jesus disciples. He was to be disciple number 13, probably to take Judas' place, but he feared losing his material possessions. Now you may wonder how this man could have been so stupid to pass up an awesome opportunity, yet many of us have experienced situations like this and responded in the same way. Have you known God was calling you to do something in life, but got scared?

I know many RHEMA graduates who had to give up careers, houses, income, friendships, etc. to attend RHEMA Bible Training Center and then pursue ministry. In my case, I also had to leave my comfort zone. For the first time in my life, I had a great job and life was simply good.

Although I knew God was calling me to attend RHEMA Bible Training Center, at first I was hesitant. I had no idea where I would work or live, much less how I would pay for tuition. My biggest problem was I had become comfortable; yet even though I was comfortable with my life, I wasn't satisfied. I knew God had bigger things in store for me.

I began to meditate on God's Word and I quickly realized that if it was God's plan, He would have to pay for it. This surely was not my plan, it was His; therefore, He was obligated to provide and pay. In less than two days after making the decision to attend RHEMA, the job and housing were provided. The first year, the money for tuition came in day by day. Everyday was faith day! There were plenty of opportunities that year to be afraid, but I continued to simply trust

God. Before the second year began, my upcoming tuition was paid in full.

In my time at RHEMA, even though my monthly paycheck was not enough to pay all of my bills, I never went without and every bill was paid. The only tuition money to ever come directly from my pocket was the initial down payment of $900; the additional $5200 came from other sources, many from people I never knew nor met. I stood in faith everyday and endured numerous trials, but God always came through. As I was faithful to give my tithes and offerings, He was always faithful in meeting my needs. I left RHEMA Bible Training Center in better physical, spiritual and financial shape than when I arrived…and God even blessed me with my beautiful wife Lacy! God authored it, God paid for it, and He even gave me extra! God is certainly good!

You see, when God gives you a mission, in most cases, it will seem impossible. Why? God always wants the glory. If it could be achieved simply through our natural abilities and talents, we could claim that we did it all by ourselves; we would get the glory instead of God. Although, when situations are accomplished through God's ability and power, He alone gets the glory and men are drawn to Him.

When God tells you to do something, through His command, He is also endowing you with the ability to accomplish the task. Yet so many times, we step out in faith only to have fear come and stop us in our tracks. The results: either we are paralyzed or we run away.

Number seven: Fear will hinder your
access to the power of God

Fearful men do not operate in the power of God. Do not think that you can be full of fear concerning a situation and still expect God to move on your behalf. You can not be in fear about your health and expect the healing power to take effect in your body. You can not be in fear about your finances and expect God to bless your pocketbook. God is not moved by pity, fear, or depression. God is moved by faith! When you get in faith, God steps in; when you get into fear, God steps out. He loves you and wants to intervene, but fear hinders God's intervention. Fear stops the power from flowing into your situation.

One example is that of Peter walking on the water. In faith, Peter walked on the water; in fear, Peter sank in the water. As long as Peter was in faith, the door to the miraculous was wide open; yet, as soon as he abandoned his faith, the door to the miraculous was slammed in his face.

In Mark 5, we are told about Jesus raising Jairus's daughter from the dead. When we read the story, we automatically focus on that one specific action: the raising from the dead. But have you ever looked at the actions which led up to this wonderful event? There were some decisions made not only by Jesus, but also by Jairus which affected the outcome of the situation. Let us begin reading with verse 35.

While He was still speaking, some came from the ruler of the synagogue's house who said, "Your daughter is dead. Why trouble the Teacher any further?" As soon as Jesus heard the word that was spoken, He said to the ruler of the synagogue, "Do not be afraid; only believe." And He permitted no one to follow Him except Peter, James, and John the brother of James. Then He came to the house of the ruler of the synagogue, and saw a tumult and those who wept and wailed loudly. When He came in, He said to them, "Why make this commotion and weep? The child is not dead, but sleeping." And they ridiculed Him. But when He had put them all outside, He took the father and the mother of the child, and those who were with Him, and entered where the child was lying. Then He took the child by the hand, and said to her, "Talitha, cumi," which is translated, "Little girl, I say to you, arise." Immediately the girl arose and walked, for she was twelve years of age. And they were overcome with great amazement.

Mark 5:35-42

When the servants reported the young girl's death, did you notice what Jesus said to Jairus? Jesus said, "Do not fear; only believe." Jesus gave him a choice and Jairus' decision would affect the life of his daughter. Jesus was basically saying, "You can choose to be afraid or to believe. If you choose to fear, you shut off My power and there is nothing I can do." Jesus could do nothing in the situation without faith on Jairus' part. In this situation, Jairus and Jesus were partners because they needed each other; Jairus had as much a part in the miracle as Jesus. Jairus' belief was like that of a control valve on a dam. Faith would release the water; fear would hold it back. In this case, Jairus kept the switch of faith turned on and refused to fear. As a result, he began the process for a miracle.

Chapter Two

The Result Of Knowledge

In Hosea 4:6, God said His people are destroyed for a lack of knowledge. In contrast, with the acquisition of knowledge, you should be a conqueror and a champion in life. God desires that we have knowledge concerning His Word. Without knowledge of our Heavenly Father and His promises, we will certainly be destroyed in life because there is an enemy who would love to see us beaten down.

If you do not have knowledge that Jesus died for your sins, how can you accept your salvation? If you do not have knowledge of your sicknesses being removed, how can you accept your healing? It doesn't take a PhD to figure out that if you do not acquire knowledge about a particular area, you will have an extremely hard time being successful in that area.

For example, if you do not have any education or training concerning bombs, would you try to disengage one? I would venture to say none of us would; although, for those who have been trained in that area, they can walk into the situation with more confidence and boldness than you or I.

Do you remember taking exams in school? The stress levels were quite different on exams in which you studied for in comparison to those in which you did not. When I was working on my master's degree, there was one test in which my study time was extremely limited; quite honestly, no studying took place. I went into that classroom sweating profusely because I knew this test could cost me severely. It is not a good thing to fail a test in graduate school! Fortunately, the test ended up being postponed and the fear I was experiencing quickly went away.

On the other hand, there was another exam in which I knew the information. I had the knowledge and I went into the classroom exuding confidence. I was not afraid, not stressed and fully confident that I would perform well; as a result, I made an "A."

What about the first day of high school? We all experienced fear and nervousness in some manner because we did not know anything about high school. We did not know where the restrooms or classrooms were, nor who our teachers were; we did not know anything. I don't know about you, but by my senior year, I walked around like I owned the school. Why? I had acquired some knowledge of where things were located and I knew all the teachers. In addition, my best friend's dad was the principal; as a result, boldness entered.

I will never forget a statement Rev. Doug Jones make. He said, "Boldness is always the result of knowledge." Looking back on situations in my life, I have seen the truth in that statement. The more you know about a situation, the bolder you are in encountering the situation.

For example, would you walk into my parent's house and get whatever you wanted out of the pantry? I do not think so. Why? You do not know my parents; therefore, you would be very timid in knocking on the door, much less helping yourself to their groceries. Although, in comparison to myself, I can walk in and go straight to the refrigerator as I say hello in passing. I have and always will have more boldness around my parents than you will. As stated earlier, boldness is a direct result of knowledge.

The first time I rode a roller coaster will always be a vivid memory. We were at an amusement park in San Antonio, Texas. At the time, this park had one of the tallest wooden roller coasters in the world. No one in my family wanted to ride it except my dad, yet somehow he talked me into riding it with him (little did I know that he was too afraid to ride it by himself!) I was fourteen years old and up to that point, I was extremely afraid of the clickety-clackety beasts. The fear I possessed had kept me from riding roller coasters up to this point in my life.

The climb up to the loading deck was tortuous. I was sweating so profusely, my shirt was thoroughly soaked; needless to say, I was terrified. By the time we reached the loading deck, we were over a hundred feet above the ground and I had already bit all my fingernails off. I almost turned back, but I saw these little kids getting off the coaster laughing; so me, my pride and my dad climbed in and held on tight.

Needless to say, after the first 170- foot nearly vertical drop and after getting my stomach out of my throat…I had a blast. The ride scared me so severely it actually scared the fear out! Upon exiting the cart, I noticed I had left my mark on the ride: the indentions of my fingers on the cart's padding!

After getting the first coaster behind me, I was ready to ride more coasters. Up to this day, I love roller coasters. Do I get scared? No, because I now have some roller coaster knowledge. I will ride anything now! With many of our fears or phobias, if we would simply face the unknown, it will become known and fear will be no more. Let us face fact: the objects and situations we are usually afraid of are those in which we have no experiential knowledge.

As I said earlier, God desires for us to be knowledgeable concerning His Word. When I say knowledgeable, I do not mean simply having head knowledge, but possessing heart knowledge. There are many well educated people in this world who possess a great deal of head knowledge concerning the Bible; yet, they have absolutely no heart knowledge concerning their Father.

God wants us to know Who He is and What He has done, is doing, and will do for us. Why? He wants us to be victorious on this earth. In relation to fear, God does not want us to live in anxiety and stress; He does not want us to have anything to do with fear. God is a faith

God and He has called us to live a faith life.

As with everything in life, God always has an answer and that answer is found in His Word. When you have God's answer to a situation, you will face that situation with confidence, with boldness and a surety that you will win. So if you are experiencing fear in your life, I encourage you to take the time and grasp the information presented in the next two chapters. If it takes reading them two or three times, by all means, please do it. This information is critical in order for you to carry out God's plan for your life.

As we have already seen, we can not be a success for God with a melted heart. All that we do, we are to do in faith because faith leads to success and victory; fear leads to disparaging failure. God wants you to be a success. He wants you to live a life of hope, courage and strength! So continue on with me as we discover God's answer for fear.

Chapter Three

The Answer
For Fear

One of my absolute favorite stories in the Bible is that of David and Goliath. Within 1 Samuel 17, David gives us a great example of the boldness we as God's people are to display. In the beginning of the chapter, we find that the Philistines and Israelites were at war; the only problem for Israel was a Philistine soldier named Goliath. (I still wonder to this day why the entire army of Israel was afraid of attacking the Philistines because of one man!)

Every day for forty days, Goliath taunted the Israelites and the Israelites did nothing. Well, one day David showed up at the camp to bring his brothers some food and overheard Goliath's blasphemous statements. Upon seeing the state of the camp, David was in disgust that the Israelites were standing back doing nothing; after all, Goliath was blaspheming the Lord God!

Well, David became irate and told King Saul he would fight Goliath. I am sure Saul took David's statement half-heartedly because David was a young shepherd boy, not a man of battle. You see, Saul was comparing David's youth and experience to that of Goliath; yet, Saul was unaware that God was with David and that David was aware of

God's abiding presence! Let's begin reading.

> David said to Saul, "Let no one lose heart on account of this Philistine;
> your servant will go and fight him." Saul replied, "You are not able
> to go out against this Philistine and fight him; you are only a boy and
> he has been a fighting man from his youth." But David said to Saul,
> "Your servant has been keeping his father's sheep. When a lion or a
> bear came and carried off a sheep from the flock, I went after it, struck
> it and rescued the sheep from its mouth. When it turned on me, I
> seized it by its hair, struck it and killed it. Your servant has killed both
> the lion and the bear; this uncircumcised Philistine will be like one of
> them, because he has defied the armies of the living God. The LORD
> who delivered me from the paw of the lion and the paw of the bear will
> deliver me from the hand of this Philistine." Saul said to David, "Go
> and the LORD be with you."
>
> 1 Samuel 17:32-37

Wow! Did you see the boldness in David's statements? Did you
see the source of David's courage? David knew God was with Him.
David had counted God faithful due to his past experiences with the
lion and the bear. God had been with David through those times and
he knew God would be with him through this situation as well.

*Boldness will cause you to run after your enemies; fear will cause
you to run from them.* I absolutely love verses 48-51 because
David's boldness turned to action. Armed with the knowledge of
God's presence, David did not wait on Goliath or sheepishly walk
towards him; David boldly ran toward his enemy and defeated
Goliath with one stone. You see, when you know God is with you,
fear is no more. David was well aware of God's presence in His
life. I submit to you this: *the remedy for fear is knowledge of God's*

presence in your life.

Now to further solidify this statement, let us look at some other examples. In Psalm 46: 1, 2 David gives us my second piece of evidence.

> **God is our refuge and strength, a very present help in trouble. Therefore, we will not fear, even though the earth be removed and though the mountains be carried into the midst of the sea.**

In my Bible, there is a study note for the phrase "*a very present help*" which states that God is "*an abundantly available help.*" Now I like that! Everything God is and does is always in abundance! Now did you notice why David said we will not fear? The answer: God is a very present, abundantly available help. Another words, we will not fear because God is with us. He is a very present help because He is within us! The answer for fear is God is here!

My third piece of evidence is found in Numbers 14. Here we find the Israelites grumbling and complaining after hearing the spies' reports of the Promised Land. They were afraid because of the giants, even though God had already given them the land. During the Israelites whining session, Caleb and Joshua responded in faith.

> **Only do not rebel against the LORD. And do not be afraid of the people of the land, because we will swallow them up. Their protection is gone, but the LORD is with us. Do not be afraid of them.**
>
> **Numbers 14:9**

Notice what they said, "Do not be afraid for the Lord is with us!" To combat the thoughts of fear, they reminded the Israelites of God's presence with them.

The children of Israel were looking at their inabilities instead of God's impossibilities; they had taken their focus off of God and placed it on their problem. Anytime your eyes become settled on the problem, you will always fail. You will never be a success without your focus on Jesus.

My fourth piece of evidence is found in Daniel 3:16-18.

> **Shadrach, Meschach, and Abednego answered and said to the king, "O Nebuchadnezzar, we have no need to answer you in this matter. Our God whom we serve is able to deliver us from the burning fiery furnace and He will deliver us from your hand O king. But if not** [if you don't throw us in] **let it be known to you, O king, that we do not serve your gods, nor will we worship the gold image which you have set up."**
>
> **Daniel 3:16-18**

Have you ever considered the boldness of Shadrach, Meschach, and Abednego? Wow! I highly respect these three men because they did not compromise their beliefs even in the face of death; yet, they were never afraid of death because they knew God was with them and would protect them. This is quite apparent in their statements of faith!

Now some say that in this verse, the three Hebrew boys were implying that *even if God didn't save them*, they would not serve the king's gods. Have you ever thought about that? That is one of the most absurd statements I have ever heard. First of all, God always delivers the righteous! He is our Deliverer and our Source of protection! Secondly - think about it - if you are dead, are you going to serve the king? Well, of course not, because you are dead! Shadrach, Meschach, and Abednego were saying if King Nebuchadnezzar *did not throw them in the furnace,* they still would not serve his gods. They were fearless in their faith that God was their Deliverer; this truth was the backbone of their two statements.

These three men were full of confidence in the situation. They knew God was with them and that belief was manifested not only in their salvation, but also in the fact that a fourth man was seen with them. God showed up!

This leads me to my fifth piece of evidence:

> During the fourth watch of the night Jesus went out to them, walking on the lake. When the disciples saw him walking on the lake, they were terrified. "It's a ghost," they said, and cried out in fear. But Jesus immediately said to them: "Take courage! It is I. Don't be afraid." "Lord if it's you," Peter replied, "tell me to come to you on the water." "Come," He said. Then Peter got down out of the boat, walked on the water and came toward Jesus. But when he saw the wind, he was afraid and, beginning to sink, cried out, "Lord, save me." Immediately Jesus reached out his hand and caught him. "You of little faith," He said, "why did you doubt?"
>
> **Matthew 14:25-31**

Now, I want to point out a few things from this passage of scripture. First of all, look at what Peter accomplished with his focus on Jesus:

he walked on water. Peter did the impossible with his faith and trust in Jesus; although, as soon as he took his eyes off Jesus and placed them on the storm, he began to sink. Remember what I said earlier? Anytime your eyes become settled on the problem, you will always fail. Yet, I am thankful that because of God's mercy, we can refocus, get back on our feet, and continue on under God's grace. Boldness will always come with your eyes on Jesus; fear will always come with your eyes on your problem.

Now remember what we are proving out: the remedy for fear is knowledge of God's presence in your life. In Matthew 14:26-27, we find my sixth piece of evidence.

> **When the disciples saw him walking on the lake, they were terrified. "It's a ghost," they said, and cried out in fear. But Jesus immediately said to them: "Take courage! It is I. Don't be afraid."**

Did you see it? What did Jesus say in response to the disciples fear? *"It is I, don't be afraid."* To combat their fear, He brought knowledge of His presence to their attention; this is why Jesus could tell them to be bold and not be afraid. Hopefully, it is becoming apparent that knowledge of God's presence is the answer to fear.

My seventh piece of evidence is found in Psalms 118:6, 7.

> **The LORD is with me; I will not be afraid. What can man do to me? The LORD is with me; He is my helper. I will look in triumph on my enemies.**

Are you starting to see it now? Why was the Psalmist not afraid?

He knew the LORD was with him! Regardless of what you are facing, fear should never be an issue. What can any man, any storm, any animal or anything else do to bring you down when the LORD Almighty is with you? With the LORD on your side, you are unstoppable. Just like David, you can look at your enemy with confidence and boldly say, "Today you will be defeated!" You can stand in victory and look in triumph over your enemies simply because God is with you.

My eighth piece of evidence is found in Isaiah 41:10.

> **Fear not, for I am with you; Be not dismayed, for I am your God. I will strengthen you, Yes, I will help you, I will uphold you with My righteous right hand.**

Again, both in the Old Testament and New Testament, God gives us the same response to fear. First of all, God commands us not to fear. Secondly, He immediately gives us the same prescription for fear: reassurance of His presence. The answer for fear is God is here!

I am sure at some point in our childhood we all had a nightmare or two growing up. When you had a bad dream and your parents woke you up, what was the first statement they would make? It was usually something like this, "It's okay. Don't be afraid. Mommy and daddy are here." You see, reassurance of their presence always had an instant calming effect.

I believe it would be safe to say this situation is almost universal and has occurred in your life either as a child or with your own children.

Actually, any time I was afraid as a child, fear instantly went away when my parents arrived on the scene. How much more confident should we be in knowing that our Heavenly Father is with us? In contrast to humanity, we don't have to wait for God to show up because He is always with us!

My ninth piece of evidence is found in John 14:15-31. Jesus is speaking to the disciples about his upcoming death, burial, and resurrection. In verse 27, Jesus told the disciples, *"Do not let your hearts be troubled, nor let them be afraid."* In the preceding verses, we see why Jesus made this statement. Do you know why? Because Jesus had just finished telling them that although He was about to leave, He was sending the Holy Spirit! No need to fear because God, by the Holy Spirit, was going to be with them!

My tenth piece of evidence is found in Acts 18:9, 10.

> **Now the Lord spoke to Paul in the night by a vision, "Do not be afraid, but speak, and do not keep silent; for I am with you, and no one will attack you to hurt you; for I have many people in this city."**

Paul was ministering in the town of Corinth and many of the Jews there were against him. Again, observe how God instills confidence in Paul; God makes the statement, *"Do not be afraid...for I am with you."* It is quite apparent that God's answer for fear is the same, regardless of the person, time, place or situation. We see God's prescription for peace like a thread woven throughout the entire Bible. The answer for fear is God is here!

My eleventh piece of evidence is 1 John 4:4.

You are of God, little children, and have overcome them because He who is in you is greater than he who is in the world.

Isn't that exciting? What Jesus promised the disciples in John 14 has now come to pass! He is not only with us, but in us! We have never truly delved into the depths of this scripture. God is in us. What an awesome truth!

Have you ever really thought about it? The Master of the universe, the Creator of all living things resides within you; therefore, wherever you go, God goes! You can go nowhere without God being with you. In any situation, He is with you. In any location, no matter how remote, He is with you. Isn't that so comforting? Our Father cannot get any closer than He already is for you are one with Him!

Our unity with our Heavenly Father is an astounding, yet wonderful truth that we must grasp and initiate in our lives. *When you realize God is with you, no fear can stay and doubt will simply fade away;* the end result is peace of mind because God is with you and nothing in this world is greater than He! Can anyone defeat God? By all means no! Then how can anyone defeat the vessel of God?

I want to show you the result of ungodliness coming against the vessel of God. In 1 Samuel 6:1-7, David and his men went to Baalah of Judah to get the Ark of the Covenant. As they were returning home with the Ark, one of the oxen stumbled which caused the Ark to fall off the cart. Uzzah reached out and grabbed hold of the Ark, but died instantly. Why? The Ark of the Covenant was the vessel of God and Uzzah was unclean. Uncleanliness has no place in God's presence nor the vessel in which He dwells.

Do you see the relevance of this story to our lives? Now we are the vessel of God, the temple of the Holy Spirit. How much more should God's living temples be protected against ungodliness than a wooden box? There is nothing in this world that can defeat you for God is in you!

You have the greatest bodyguard in Heaven and on earth. God is with you and He has never been defeated; He has never lost a battle. Every fight He has fought has been an immediate knockout! How could you ever be afraid with a bodyguard like that? Through the apostle John, God not only tells us He is greater than anything in the world, but that He is also in us. What a wonderful and life changing truth! Praise God!

My twelfth and final piece of evidence is found in Joshua 1:5, 9.

> **As I was with Moses, I will be with you; I will never leave you nor forsake you. Do not fear or be discouraged, for the Lord will be with you wherever you go.**

We see God preparing Joshua for his time of leadership and giving him instruction. God's way of instilling confidence and dispelling fear was reminding Joshua of His presence. From that point on, Joshua fulfilled his God given purpose in absolute victory knowing that God was with him. You too can go forth and fulfill your God given purpose and yet go with even more confidence than Joshua. Why? Let us read Joshua 1:5, 9 in the context of being a new covenant Christian.

> **I will never leave you, nor forsake you. Do not fear or be discouraged, for the Lord will be** [in you] **wherever you go.**

Glory to God! He is in us wherever we go; there is no place we can go that our Heavenly Father will not be with us!

It simply does not matter what situation you are facing or the circumstances you are going through. Whether you have just received a bad report from the doctor or you are facing foreclosure, the answer is the same. Whether you can't pay your bills or a gun is pointed to your head, the answer is the same. Whether your spouse just left you or a loved one has died, the answer is still the same. Whether a tornado is headed your way or you are locked away in prison, the answer does not change. Knowledge of God's presence in your life will obliterate every fear, every concern, every doubt, and every stress that may try to attack you. This knowledge is your shield of faith concerning fear. Armed with this profound and powerful truth, you are setting the course for a life free of fear. *The answer for fear: God is here!*

Chapter Four

The Identity
Of Fear

I believe that sufficient evidence has been given to establish that the answer for fear is knowledge of God's presence in your life. Although, in order to deal with the issue of fear and to live a fearless life, we must know what fear is so we can deal with it appropriately. For example, in the military, before they go to battle, the leader must have some knowledge about their enemy so they will know how to fight and what type of weapons to use. Without knowledge of who your enemy is, the battle is already lost for no strategy can be devised.

So, what is fear? Through much religion, tradition, and one scripture, the Church has been taught and has accepted the teaching that fear is a spirit.

> **For God did not give us a spirit of fear, but a spirit of power, love and a sound mind.**
>
> **2 Timothy 1:7**

Now anyone with any type of biblical schooling knows that you cannot and must not allow one scripture to form a belief. Jesus said in Matthew 18:16, *"By the mouth of two or three witnesses shall every word be established."* If there is a truth presented in the Bible, there will always be at least a second scripture to back it up; yet, you will never find another scripture declaring fear as a spirit.

From this scripture, if we assume that fear is a spirit, we must also assume that power, love, and a sound mind are spirits because this scripture is portraying a comparison of opposites. Now let me ask you some questions. Is power a spirit? Is love a spirit? Is a sound mind or self control a spirit? The answer is no, no, and no. Actually, in Galatians 5:22, we find that love and self control (sound mind) are fruits or characteristics of the Holy Spirit and our recreated spirit. We also can see throughout the Bible that power is a characteristic of the Holy Spirit. So, if these three items are not spirits, then fear can not be a spirit.

CHARACTERISTICS OF TWO SPIRITS

Within 2 Timothy 1:7 are simply characteristics of two spirits; Paul is simply giving us personality traits of the Holy Spirit and Satan. Fear is a trait of Satan; power, love and a sound mind are traits of the Holy Spirit and our recreated spirit. For you English majors, these are simply adjectives describing a noun. To help you out, allow me to change the nouns and adjectives to really make this clear. What if I gave you a car and I said, "I have not given you a junky car, but a car that is new, powerful, and luxurious." What am I doing? I am comparing two cars; I am comparing characteristics of two vehicles.

In this verse, Paul was not defining or identifying fear; he was simply describing the Holy Spirit God has given us. Timothy was experiencing some very difficult times as pastor of his church. Because of this, Paul was trying to instill confidence and boldness in Timothy. Did you notice how Paul was instilling confidence and dispelling fear? He was doing it just like God and just like Jesus: he was reminding Timothy of God's abiding presence. Remember, the answer for fear is God is here!

As I was teaching along these lines, I had a woman ask me, "Since fear is not a spirit, can I no longer quote 2 Timothy 1:7 when I am afraid?" I explained to her that, yes, she should still quote it, but now to say it with the newfound knowledge and understanding of that verse. Confess 2 Timothy 1:7 for the same reason that Paul wrote it: to remind yourself of the great and mighty God that is living within you!

FEAR IS NOT A SPIRIT

If we look at 2 Timothy 1:7 in its context and in comparison to what the rest of the Bible says, we see very plainly that fear is not a spirit. Now you may say, "Does it really matter if fear is a spirit or a belief?" Absolutely! *The identity of your enemy will determine your weaponry.* As we will later see, we do not handle evil spirits in the same manner as ungodly beliefs.

Based on multiple scriptures throughout the Bible, I am firmly persuaded that fear is simply a belief and I will endeavor to prove this to you by the Word of God. I believe that as we search the scriptures, this truth will quickly become visible to you.

Let us begin reading Matthew 8:23-27 in the Amplified Version.

> **And after He got into the boat, His disciples followed Him. And suddenly, behold, there arose a violent storm on the sea, so that the boat was being covered up by the waves; but He was sleeping. And they went and awakened Him, saying, Lord, rescue and preserve us! We are perishing! And He said to them, Why are you timid and afraid, O you of little faith? Then He got up and rebuked the winds and the sea, and there was a great and wonderful calm (a perfect peaceableness). And the men were stunned with bewildered wonder and marveled, saying, What kind of Man is this, that even the winds and the sea obey Him!**

Now, I want you to notice a few things regarding the issue of fear's identity. First of all, who did Jesus address, the disciples or an evil spirit? He addressed the disciples. Notice that He didn't say, "Why did you allow that spirit of fear to overtake you?" or "I rebuke that spirit of fear." If an evil spirit was present, do you not think Jesus would have dealt with it? Instead, He dealt with the disciples as if their being fearful was their responsibility.

I find it interesting that in the following verses of Matthew 8:28-34, immediately after this incident on the water, Jesus is presented with two demon-possessed men and He cast out the evil spirits. Now compare both situations: *When the disciples were fearful, Jesus dealt with the disciples' faith, not an evil spirit. When the two men were demon-possessed, Jesus dealt with the evil spirits, not the men.*

So in the boat, did a spirit of fear suddenly jump on the disciples and then jump off? I think not. According to this passage of scripture, the responsibility fell on the disciples; Jesus said it was due to their faith.

> And when the disciples saw Him walking on the sea, they were terrified and said, It is a ghost! And they screamed with fright. But instantly He spoke to them, saying, Take courage! I AM! Stop being afraid! And Peter answered Him, Lord, if it is You, command me to come to You on the water. He said, Come! So Peter got out of the boat and walked on the water and he came toward Jesus. But when he perceived the waves and the wind became strong, he was frightened, and as he began to sink, he cried out, Lord, save me! Instantly, Jesus reached out His hand and caught and held him saying, O you of little faith, why did you doubt?
>
> **Matthew 14:28-31**

There are two points in this story I would like to bring to your attention. First, notice Jesus responded to Peter's belief and not an evil spirit. Are you getting this now? Fear is not a spirit, but a belief.

Did you see how Jesus calmed their fears? He combated the fearful thoughts with acknowledgement of His presence. The answer for fear is God is here! He did not just say, "It's me Jesus." No, He said, "I AM!" Another words, God is here!

Secondly, look at His last three words: "Stop being afraid." The subject in this sentence is the understood "You" or the person to whom the phrase is being directed. The disciples were the understood subjects of this sentence. Notice, He rebuked the disciples and their beliefs, not an evil spirit.

Did you ever see Jesus tell some of the demon possessed people to stop being possessed? No, because an evil spirit was causing the problem. Jesus told the disciples to stop being afraid because it was their responsibility to control their beliefs; Jesus dealt with the men and not an evil spirit. The disciples were the only ones with authority over their minds. Fearful thoughts came as a result of what they saw and every last one of them grabbed hold of those thoughts and got into fear. Are you seeing it? Fear is not a spirit, but a belief.

Have you ever had someone walk up behind you and scare you? Have you ever been sitting on your couch and seen a little mouse run across the floor? When you screamed in fright, was that a spirit of fear jumping on you? I think not!

My wife Lacy used to be an easy one to scare. I could jump out from behind a corner and she would jump and scream; yet when she saw me, she would no longer be scared. Then, she would turn around and I would sneak up on her again and get the same results. Does that mean a spirit of fear jumped on her, left, jumped back on her and then left again? Nope, she temporarily abandoned her beliefs. Fear is not a spirit, but simply a belief.

I can remember a number of times in the past in which I had been balancing our checkbook and came up short.   Seeing the negative balance, I would get pretty worried, so I would recheck my numbers; thankfully, I usually found a mistake or two. When I recalculated my numbers, I was back in the black and the stress was gone. Did that mean a spirit of fear came on me? No, I was merely putting more trust in my checkbook than in God's Word. Red or black numbers - God's Word is still the same.   It was my fault for not standing strong on God's promises of provision regardless of the figures in my checkbook.

My third example is Luke 24:36-39 (Amplified):

> **Now while they were talking about this, Jesus Himself took His stand among them and said to them, Peace (freedom from all the distresses that are experienced as the result of sin) be to you! But they were so startled and terrified that they thought they saw a spirit. And He said to them, Why are you disturbed and troubled and why do such doubts and questionings arise in your hearts? See My hands and My feet, that it is I Myself! Feel and handle Me and see, for a spirit does not have flesh and bones, as you see that I have.**

As we have seen before, Jesus once again calms their fears by getting them to acknowledge or become aware of His presence.

I want to draw your attention to the question Jesus asked the disciples. He said, *"Why are you disturbed and troubled and why do such questionings and doubts arise in your hearts?"* Jesus reveals to us that their fears, worries and concerns were a direct result as to what was in their heart, not an evil spirit. We believe with our heart and confess with our mouth our beliefs. The disciples had confessed the fear in their hearts and Jesus verbally spanked them for it.

Finally, I would like to examine the story of Jairus found in Luke 8.

And behold, there came a man named Jairus, and he was a ruler of the synagogue. And he fell down at Jesus' feet and begged Him to come to his house, for he had an only daughter about twelve years of age, and she was dying... While He was still speaking, someone came from the ruler of the synagogue's house, saying to him, Your daughter is dead. Do not trouble the Teacher. But when Jesus heard it, He answered him say, Do not be afraid; only believe, and she will be made well.

Luke 8:41, 42, 49, 50

There are two things I would like to point out. Number one, again, Jesus contrasts fear and faith. Jesus knew that due to the death report, Jairus could become fearful; yet notice Jesus did not respond to a "spirit of fear," but responded to Jairus' beliefs. Jesus, in His compassion, tried to help Jairus keep the switch of faith turned on. By His statements, we see that Jairus' beliefs were the central focus. Jairus' decision to stay in faith or move into fear was at stake; his decision would also be the determining factor in his daughter's fate.

Number two, we see that Jairus had a choice: he could remain in faith or step into fear. Jesus presented Jairus with a choice when He said, *"Do not be afraid; only believe..."* It reminds me of a statement God made to the Israelites:

...I have set before you life and death, blessing and cursing; therefore choose life, that both you and your descendants may live.

Deuteronomy 30:19

Essentially, Jesus made the same statement to Jairus. The life and death of Jairus' daughter was set before him; for Jairus to choose life, he had to choose faith. As God had no control over the Israelites choice, Jesus had no control over Jairus's choice.   Jesus had no authority over Jairus' thoughts or his beliefs; the only one who could control the situation was Jairus.   Our being in fear or faith is under our control. *We have a choice: to be afraid or believe.*

In each example, Jesus did not deal with a "spirit of fear," but He dealt with the people.   Each time, He places the blame on the people and each time it is a question of their faith.   Did you notice the repetitive language Jesus used in each situation: "Why do you doubt," "You of little faith," "Where is your faith?" "Why do you question in your heart?"   In summary, Jesus said it was a condition of their faith.

Well, what is faith? Faith can be defined as a conviction, a persuasion, a firm persuasion, or a belief.   Faith is trust in God; fear is trust in everything else.   In order for Jesus to work the supernatural in the people's lives, fear had to be eradicated; faith had to be present.   In order to rid the people's fear, Jesus had to help them change their beliefs; but for this to occur, *He had to change and refocus their thinking.*

Chapter Five

Knock, Knock

Now that we have established what fear is, we need to understand how fear comes. Since all beliefs are formed in the same manner, let us first look at how faith comes.

Romans 10:17 says, "Faith comes by hearing and hearing by the Word of God." When we hear the Word or see the Word, faith comes. The more we begin to meditate and dwell on the Word, the more the Word becomes a part of us. In this way, God's beliefs become our beliefs.

Our beliefs are formed by what we see or hear; in a sense, you become what you behold. Likewise, fear also comes by what you see and hear. Therefore, there are two doors through which fear comes: your eyes and ears.

And the LORD spoke to Moses, saying, Send men to spy out the land of Canaan, which I am giving to the children of Israel...they brought back word to them and to all the congregation, and showed them the fruit of the land. They told them, We went to the land where you sent us. It truly flows with milk and honey and this is its fruit. Nevertheless the people who dwell in the land are strong; the cities are fortified and very large; moreover we saw the descendants of Anak there. So all

the congregation lifted up their voices and cried, and the people wept that night.

Numbers 13:1, 2, 27, 28, & 14:1

It is interesting that the spies were confident they could take the land until they saw the giants and fortified cities; the rest of the Israelites were confident until they heard the fear filled report from the spies. The report was based on fear and consequently, the hearts of the people melted.

So why did their hearts melt? The spies were afraid because of what they saw and the rest were afraid because of what they heard; consequently, they all backed out of faith and backed into fear. With the exception of Joshua and Caleb, the Israelites failed to claim what God had given them.

With your mindset on God, you can do all things; with your mindset on your circumstances, you can do nothing. To make it very plain, fear is trusting in your circumstances; faith is trusting in God despite your circumstances. When you choose to stop trusting in God, fear is the automatic result. There is no grey area in this; it is simply black or white. If you are not in faith, you are in fear.

Another example I would like to look at is found in 2 Kings 6. The king of Syria was trying to kill Elisha because he was causing problems in the king's efforts to defeat Israel. One day, Elisha's servant went out of their house and saw a great army of chariots and horses surrounding the city and he became frightened.

And when the servant of the man of God arose early and went out, there was an army, surrounding the city with horses and chariots. And his servant said to him, Alas, my master! What shall we do?

2 Kings 6:15, 16

Notice the servant was not afraid or concerned until he saw something; fear came when he saw the great Syrian army. Elisha's response to his fear is wonderful:

So he answered, Do not fear, for those who are with us are more than those who are with them. And Elisha prayed, and said, Lord, I pray, open his eyes that he may see. Then the LORD opened the eyes of the young man, and he saw. And behold, the mountain was full of horses and chariots of fire all around Elisha.

2 Kings 6:17, 18

It is wonderful to know that even when it seems you are outnumbered, the reality is you are not! It brings such great peace to know that God and my angels are always with me! If I was a betting man, I would bet that servant quickly became extremely confident in the outcome of the situation. Why? He saw that God was with them! As faith comes, fear comes: by what you see and hear.

Earlier in our study, we read the story of Jesus and Peter walking on the water. There is another point in this story I would like to bring to your attention in regards to how fear comes.

And when the disciples saw Him walking on the sea, they were terrified and said, It is a ghost! And they screamed with fright. But instantly He spoke to them, saying, Take courage! I AM! Stop being afraid!

Matthew 14:26-27 Amplified

Notice the disciples did not become afraid until they saw something. The disciples thought they were seeing a ghost and began screaming like a bunch of babies; although, I find it so compassionate of Jesus that at the sound of their screaming, He instantly calmed their fears.

Remember what I said earlier? Fear comes as a result of what you see or hear. The disciples saw and became afraid. Now look at what happened to Peter in verse 28-31:

> **And Peter answered Him, Lord, if it is You, command me to come to You on the water. He said, Come! So Peter got out of the boat and walked on the water and he came toward Jesus. But when he perceived the waves and the wind became strong, he was frightened, and as he began to sink, he cried out, Lord, save me! Instantly, Jesus reached out His hand and caught and held him saying, O you of little faith, why did you doubt?**
>
> **Matthew 14:28-31**

Peter fearlessly stepped out of the boat and began his faith walk toward Jesus; although as soon as Peter began to look at the waves, he became scared again. Peter allowed his flesh to dictate his thoughts and became afraid. His sight led to a fearful thought which led to a fearful belief and consequently, led to a fearful result.

What you believe is determined by what you think; what you think is determined by what you see and hear. (This should be a lesson to you to always keep your eyes on the Answer and not the problem.) So on the water, the disciples went from being unafraid to being afraid to unafraid to being afraid to unafraid - all based on what they saw and heard - and this happened within a matter of minutes!

Fear is not a spirit that jumps on you like a cat on a mouse; fear is a belief and that belief comes from what you see and hear. As faith comes, fear comes - by what you behold.

Now let's look at some personal examples. Have you ever seen a shadow on your window at night? Many of us as children experienced seeing a person with scraggly arms and hands in our windows. You would see that nasty person's shadow and it was really scary; although, the fear did not subside until we pulled the curtains back and realized it was a tree.

Another example we can all relate to is that of seeing flashing red and blue lights in our rear view mirror. I don't know about you, but I have never had a feeling of peace or joy when I see those lights. Even if I haven't done anything wrong, my heart immediately starts pounding and I break out in a cold sweat (it's probably due to all the speeding tickets I received in college!) It is only when the police car passes by and pulls someone else over that the fear subsides! I think I can safely say I am not the only person like that; I am sure you have acted in the same manner!

Did you like that example? Well, if that didn't help, then here is yet another. It is quite humorous now, but when I was in fourth grade, it was not funny. I was ten years old and it was a Saturday morning. I was asleep in my bed when I heard a loud trumpet blast. I jumped out of my bed and I heard a second trumpet blast. My little brother Justin wasn't in his bed, so I started searching the rooms to find the source of the trumpet blast; I was tired and I wanted to go back to sleep! Well, as I searched the house, I could not find any of my family. Again, I heard a trumpet blast. By this time, I started to get very, very afraid. Why?

Well, a few weeks before, I had attended a church lock-in and we had watched a movie about the rapture; in the beginning of the movie, there was an angel blowing a trumpet announcing Jesus' return. All of the scenes that followed the rapture would have scared any adult, much less a kid in fourth grade!

Well, when I heard those three trumpet blasts and could not find any of my family in the house, I was petrified; I thought I had been left behind! Remembering what happened in the movie, I was trying to be strong and face the fact I was left for the tribulation when I looked into the backyard and saw my little sister Jamie by some of our pear trees. I figured, "I guess she got left too!"

I was so excited I wasn't left alone (never mind the fact that she was to face the tribulation as well!) So, I opened the back door and ran out toward the pear trees. When I got nearer, I saw my mom and dad picking pears with Jamie. Justin was also with them - blowing a trumpet my uncle had given us! I sure was glad to know it was Justin blowing the trumpet and not an angel. Fear came with the sound of a trumpet blast and left when I saw my family was still on the earth. Needless to say, the rapture didn't happen that day!

Did you notice in all of these examples that fear and faith came in through the same doors? *Your eyes and ears are doors through which information enters and what you do with that information is determined by the knowledge you possess.*

FEED YOUR FAITH, NOT YOUR FEARS

This is why it is so important that you be extremely cautious as to what you listen to and watch. Regardless of whether it is a movie, cartoon, romance novel, magazine or religious book, consider what you are beholding. Whatever you allow to come through your ears and eyes will surely affect you.

I do not watch horror shows anymore. I used to watch them growing up because I liked the suspense; I did not see the harm in them. Yet, after every movie, I would be afraid to be at home by myself or be in the dark. Every little sound at night would make me think someone was trying to break in the house and I would have a horrible time trying to sleep. Why? I had watched something I should not have watched and as a result, it was affecting me in a negative way. I think you can honestly say that my post-movie actions were not those of a man of faith! No, they were the actions of a faithless, fear-filled wimp.

For some reason when I was growing up, people all around me would tell me not to watch certain movies because it contained sex or cursing, but never said anything about the horror flicks; in my opinion, the fear filled movies are just as bad. Why? They dominate you! In Christ, I am more than a conqueror (Romans 8:37) and I refuse to be dominated by anything except the Word of God.

Watching all that garbage feeds the fear and the more you eat of it, the fatter you get. We are to be faith giants, not fear giants. It is time we watch what we eat! Start feeding your faith with the Word of God and solid Bible based teaching. Just as fear can be strengthened in your life, so can your faith. You are what you behold my friend. Feed your faith and starve out the fear!

Please consider what you are listening to and what you are watching. Ask yourself, "Is this lifting me up or pushing me down?" "Is this content empowering me or weakening me?" In short, is it feeding your faith? If not, get rid of it now! *Fear and faith come through the same door; it is up to you who enters your home.*

Chapter Six

Mind Control

In the book of Philippians, we find a wonderful passage of scripture which summarizes most of what we have discussed so far. Let's read Philippians 4:6-8 together.

> **Do not fret or have any anxiety about anything, but in every circumstance and in everything, by prayer and petition with thanksgiving, continue to make your wants known to God. And God's peace which transcends all understanding shall mount guard over your hearts and minds in Christ Jesus. For the rest, brethren, whatever is true, whatever is just, whatever is pure, whatever is lovely, whatever is kind, if there is any virtue and excellence, if there is anything worthy of praise, think on these things.**

There are some key points I want you to see in this passage. First of all, we are told not to fear; it is a command, not an option. Notice, it is up to us not to fear, worry, or be stressed because we have control over these areas.

Secondly, we are told what to do when we face a negative situation: we bring it to God. 1 Peter 5:7 says to cast all of our worries upon the Lord and this is what Paul is saying here in his letter to the Philippians. When a fearful or stressful situation arises, give it to your Heavenly Father and then thank Him for the victory. There is no sense in you worrying about it, so let God handle it; but, notice you still have to do something. You have to make the choice not to fear, you have to give the situation over to God, and you have to praise Him in faith.

So what are the results of these actions? The peace of God manifests in your life. I like what the Amplified Version of Philippians 4:7 says, *"...and the peace of God shall mount guard and garrison over your heart and mind."* The peace of God will be like an armed soldier standing guard over your heart and mind! It is a wonderful experience to have peace regarding a trial, but that does not mean the peace will stay. Now, I am sure some of you are asking, "Well, why not?" I am glad you asked.

KEEPING THE PEACE

As with anything, what is gained can quickly be lost. Spiritually or naturally, in most cases, just because you have something does not mean that it can't be taken away. Now let me clear something up real quick - God never gives and takes away. People have taken what Job said in Job 1:21 and made another doctrine out of it. When you get to Heaven, go ask Job about that statement and I guarantee you, he will tell you how wrong that statement was.

Understand, everything in the Bible is truly stated, although not everything stated is true. There are statements by Satan and ungodly men and women in the Bible. Does that make them true? No, but they are truly stated. In this case, Job is simply speaking from ignorance in an extremely traumatic situation. In comparison with the rest of the Word of God, we know Job's statement is not true, yet it is widely spoken and even sung in our churches. This is why it is so important to know who is doing the talking and to fully understand the context of the scripture as well as how it relates to the Bible as a whole.

Anything God gives you, it is meant to be kept forever. God's gifts are like his Word - everlasting, eternal, forever - yet you have the entire responsibility of determining whether you keep the gift activated in your life or not. Whether it is faith, joy, healing, prosperity, favor, or peace, you determine the length of the manifestation in your life.

Acts 10:38 tells us Satan will steal, kill and destroy if you allow him. Jesus gave an example of Satan's actions in His parable of the sower.

> **The sower sows the word. And these are the ones by the wayside where the word is sown. When they hear, Satan comes immediately and takes away the word that was sown in their hearts.**
>
> **Mark 4:14, 15**

Satan does not want you to obtain the promises of God. If he can not stop you from receiving, he will try to stop you from maintaining. The Word of God is the basis of God's blessings, including peace. Satan does not want you to be at peace; that is why he sends fearful thoughts in the first place. Be assured, Satan is the thief, not God; God does not give and take away. My Heavenly Father is strictly a bountiful giver!

So how can you lose the peace of God? The answer: your thought life. Have you ever noticed that after you make a decision to stand in faith regarding a certain situation, Satan will return with negative thoughts about that situation? For example, let us say that you prayed for healing in your body. As soon as you prayed in faith, you were at peace and full of joy. All of a sudden, here come thoughts like: "God didn't hear you!" "You are wasting your time because you don't have enough faith!" "This healing business isn't for today!" "You can't get healed because you are a sorry old sinner!" You know what I am talking about; we have all experienced it.

The reason Satan brings those thoughts is because he wants you dwell on fear and defeat. As soon as you let go of your faith, you open the door to Satan. Satan now has free reign to take what was given to you. Thank God that Paul's instructions in Philippians 4 did not stop with verse 7. In verse 8, he gives us instructions on how to rest and maintain the peace of God.

> **For the rest, brethren, whatever is true, whatever is just, whatever is pure, whatever is lovely, whatever is kind, if there is any virtue and excellence, if there is anything worthy of praise, think on these things.**

Do you see it? Look at the first three words: *for the rest.* Do you want to rest and continue to rest? Think on the Word! Faith is always at rest; fear is always stressed. After we give God our cares, thank Him for the victory and receive the peace, we must do one other thing: control our thoughts. In Colossians 3:1-3, Paul states:

If then you were raised with Christ, seek those things which are above, where Christ is, sitting at the right hand of God. Set your mind on things above, not on things on the earth. For you died and your life is hidden with Christ in God.

Again, we are told to set our minds on the higher things. Why? Our life is in Christ. All that God has given us is in Him, including peace! The end result of keeping our minds on Christ will always be peace.

According to 2 Corinthians 5:17, when you accept Christ, you become a new creature and the life of God floods your being. The life of God is in you, but to partake of the benefits, one of which is peace, you must meditate on it. We must do as Paul instructed Timothy:

Do not neglect the gift that is in you...meditate on these things; give yourself entirely to them, that your progress may be evident to all.
1 Timothy 4:14, 15

In the context of this passage, Paul was talking about Timothy's ministry gift, but it can scripturally be applied to any spiritual gift God has given us. One of those gifts is peace. Therefore, if we want the peace of God to be manifest and evident in our life, we must continually keep our minds on God and His Word; this is how we not only manifest the peace of God, but maintain it as well.

Philippians 4:6-8 is a step by step instruction guide to receiving and keeping the answers to your prayers. It applies to finances, healing, deliverance, etc; every promise you find in the Word, this is how you get it and keep it. Because this passage of scripture is so important, I have listed the key points below.

1. *We are commanded not to fear. Again, notice it is up to us not to fear or worry; we have control over what enters our mind and what stays in our mind.*
2. *When we place our trust in God by turning over our concerns to Him with thanksgiving, His peace will mount guard over our hearts and minds. Once more, it is up to us to do something.*
3. *If we want to keep the peace of God, we must continue to think on the Word. Again, we must do something.*
4. *In summary, if you want verse 7, you must do verse 6. If you want to keep verse 7, you must do verse 8.*

We have a responsibility to keep what God has provided for us. God has given us instructions; therefore, we can not blame Him when peace leaves. I believe the number one reason we as Christians lose God's blessings in our lives is because we abandon our beliefs. We begin to get our mind off of God's Word and get our mind on Satan's word. We let go of His promises and grab hold of Satan's lies.

DON'T ABANDON THE WORD

You see, you can't date the Word; you are to be married to it! Come good times and bad times, you do not leave. Jesus made a vow to us and we have made a vow to Him. Jesus said He would never leave us nor forsake us, yet how many times do we abandon His Word because of what we see or hear?

> **Now it happened, on a certain day that He got into a boat with His disciples. And He said to them, Let us cross over to the other side of the lake. And they launched out. But as they sailed He fell asleep. And a windstorm came down on the lake, and they were filling with water, and were in jeopardy. And they came to Him and awoke Him, saying, Master, Master, we are perishing! Then He arose and rebuked the wind and the raging of the water. And they ceased, and there was calm. But He said to them, Where is your faith? And they were afraid, and marveled, saying to one another, Who can this be? For He commands even the winds and water, and they obey Him!**
>
> **Luke 8:22-25**

The disciples had His word, yet when they saw the waves and heard the wind, they became afraid. The disciples should have continued to dwell on Jesus' statement, *"...Let us cross over to the other side of the lake."* Instead, they abandoned Jesus' word and began trusting in their circumstances. As a result, their hearts were melted and their courage was gone. How sad that their confidence was in the waves instead of Jesus' word.

I used to be afraid of flying on airplanes; I admit it, I was a scaredy cat. I knew God's promises about protection, but when I would get on an airplane, the knowledge of those promises never boarded the plane with me! I continually abandoned the Word on airplanes! But one day I got a hold of what Jesus said to the disciples, "Let us cross over to the other side," and I began applying it to my life; now, I fly all over the world and I simply enjoy every trip.

When I step onto an airplane, I simply say, "Let's cross on over to …" wherever I am flying and I don't think anything else about it. Why? Number one, I am making a statement of faith. I am taking control of the situation by declaring what is going to happen because I will have what I say (Proverbs 18:20-21). Number two, it simply reminds me that it is not only me crossing over, but God with me - for He is in me! I remind myself of His presence! Peace settles in and fear has no room to stay.

Simply put, if you had peace about a situation and the peace is gone, you abandoned the Word of God concerning the situation. If you were in faith, but now in fear, you have abandoned your knowledge of God's presence in your life and are not thinking on the Word, but your situation.

Now don't slump your shoulders and get sad. I have good news for you: you can pick up where you left off! If you were walking along and dropped a large amount of money, what would you do? Would you continue to stand there and sulk because you dropped it or would you pick it back up? You would most certainly pick the money back up.

Rejoice, for you can pick your peace back up if you lost it. You can pick your healing back up if you dropped it. Grab hold of the Word of God and begin meditating on the promises. Begin meditating on the reality that God is with you! Begin meditating on the truth that you are healed by the stripes of Jesus! The promise of God you mediate on will be the promise that manifests in your life and as long as you continue to dwell on the promise, it will stay in your life.

AUTHORITY OVER YOUR THOUGHT LIFE

Fear comes from faulty thinking. If fear were a spirit, you could command it to be gone in the Name of Jesus; yet, the Name of Jesus has no control over your thoughts or fearful beliefs. *There is one person who has authority over the contents of your heart and your mind...and that person is you!* After all, we have been taught that the name of Jesus has authority over everything, but this teaching is completely wrong.

Now pick yourself up off the floor and don't call me a blasphemer yet. I know it may be quite a shock to you, but in order to have the results of the Bible, we must live according to the Bible and not religious teaching. Some teaching sounds spiritual, but that does not qualify it as truth.

Here is a wonderful Bible truth for you to grab hold of ...are you ready? *If the death, burial and resurrection of Jesus Christ did not conquer it, then His name does not have authority over it.* The death, burial and resurrection of Jesus Christ did not conquer your thought life; therefore, you cannot "In the Name of Jesus" your thoughts.

Honestly, how many times in the past has an ungodly thought come to your mind and you quickly responded, "In the Name of Jesus be gone!" and the thought was still there? Then you kept repeating and repeating the Name and the thought just continued to pitch its tent.

Have you ever wondered why that occurred without any results? Was it a lack of faith? No, it was simply a lack of authority. *The problem was that you were trying to use Jesus' authority; yet, He has no authority over your thoughts.*

Here is another very important truth you must capture. *If Jesus did not have authority over something in His earthly ministry, His name does not either!* Throughout the Gospels, we see Jesus use His authority over sickness, disease, demons, winds, waves, and even death; yet, Jesus never had the authority to change the people's thoughts or beliefs. Remember, God gave us a free will; He cannot usurp our will.

If Jesus had control over people's wills, then we could command someone to get saved "In the Name of Jesus" and expect someone to be instantly saved. If Jesus had control over the will of people, we could command a particular individual to marry us in Jesus' name. If that were the case, you know there would be some really ugly guys with some really good looking women and vice versa! Sadly enough, people really try to do this!

As Jesus had no control over the will of a person, He also had no control over the thought life of a person; your thought life and your will are a package. If Jesus had control over fearful thoughts, why did He not control the disciples' fearful thoughts? How come He did not change their thoughts? The answer is that He had no control over their mind. His only avenue was to teach them how to renew their minds with knowledge of God's presence. This is why Romans

12:2 tells us to renew our minds. We cannot pray for God to renew our minds nor can we command our minds to be renewed "In the Name of Jesus." We are to renew our minds by spending time in the Word. We control our thoughts.

I would like to draw your attention to Matthew 6:31-34.

> **Therefore do not worry, saying 'What shall we eat?' or 'What shall we drink?' or 'What shall we wear?' For after all these things the Gentiles seek. For your heavenly Father knows that you need all these things. But seek first the kingdom of God and His righteousness and all these things shall be added to you. Therefore do not worry about tomorrow, for tomorrow will worry about its own things. Sufficient for the day is its own trouble.**

This familiar passage of scripture contains an extremely important truth concerning our thoughts. One Sunday morning, the minister was using this passage concerning faith, but the Holy Spirit opened it up to me in a totally different way. God and His Word are so amazing! The Word is alive. We can read the same verse over and over and always receive new revelation!

Well, concerning this passage, I got a new revelation. Now, you may look at Matthew 6:33 and still not understand the correlation of the verse and our subject, so let me explain it to you. Remember, we are talking about the correlation of our thought life and fear. Essentially, in this passage, as in Philippians 4:6-8, we are given the prescription for getting rid of fearful thoughts. As Christians, we are told not to worry, but to "seek first the kingdom of God and His righteousness." In order for you to seek after something, you must be thinking about it. Your actions are preceded by your thoughts; what you are dwelling upon is what you will do.

So how do you seek after the kingdom of God and His righteousness? Your starting point is thinking about the kingdom of God and His righteousness. You do not start seeking until you start thinking. Another words, if you do not want fearful, worry-filled thoughts, you must revert your thinking to heavenly things, otherwise you will step into fear.

We must bring our minds into subjection to the Word of God. *What you do is a direct result of what you think upon; your actions are preceded by your considerations.* If you think fear, you will act in fear. If you think on God's Word, you will act on God's Word.

If you want Bible results, you must follow Bible instructions. Do not expect to attain God's promises without following God's directions; it simply does not work that way. The Bible tells us to think on heavenly things in order to have peace, not to "In the Name of Jesus" your thoughts. Using His Name sounds very spiritual, but it is not what our Heavenly Father instructed us to do regarding our thoughts.

JESUS OUR EXAMPLE

At the Garden of Gethsemane, Jesus gave us the greatest example in the Bible of controlling one's thought life in regards to fear. Jesus faced many trials, but none compared to that of dying on the cross.

In Matthew 26:36-46, we find Jesus in the Garden struggling with the physical and spiritual death which was drawing near. Jesus told the disciples that the spirit is willing, but the flesh is weak. Three times Jesus prayed, *"O Father, if this cup cannot pass away from Me unless I drink it, Your will be done."* It is easy to see that Jesus was having a war with His mind and His flesh; He was experiencing a serious battle.

The weight of His crucifixion was bearing down on Him so severely that He began sweating blood. He had a tremendous amount of pressure on Him and had a prime opportunity to be afraid; yet, He never cast away a "spirit of fear." If fear were an evil spirit, I certainly think Jesus would have sent it packing that day!

The point I want you to see is that in the midst of fear, stress, and anxiety, Jesus was trying to maintain His thought life. He had to shift His thoughts from the natural to the spiritual; He had to focus on the Heavenly things instead of the earthly things. Jesus made a choice to think about His Father's will; thus, He was able to maintain His obedience to God and defeat fear.

I can still hear Kenneth E. Hagin saying, "You can't keep the birds from flying over your head, but you can keep them from building a nest." You cannot stop the thoughts from coming, but you can control what you think and the thoughts on which you meditate.

> **Casting down arguments and every high thing that exalts itself against the knowledge of God, bringing every thought into captivity to the obedience of Christ.**
>
> **2 Corinthians 10:5**

This is exactly what Jesus did in the Garden of Gethsemane. He was being tempted with fear, so He got into the presence of God and took the fearful thoughts captive with God's Word. Jesus told Peter in Matthew 26:41, *"Pray so that you do not enter into temptation."* We have a responsibility to follow Jesus' example and this is accomplished by getting into the Word and bringing your thought life into subjection to the Word. Where light is, darkness can not be!

We need to also follow Jesus' example during His time of testing in the wilderness. When fear comes to your door, declare, "It is written..." and complete it with a scripture covering your case. Remind the devil and remind yourself of God's promises. You do not "In the Name of Jesus" your thoughts! You are to fill your mind with what is written in the Word of God! Get into His Word! Get into His presence! Fill your heart and mind with His Word and declare it in faith!

Do not allow fearful thoughts to be exalted above God's Word. When you allow those fearful thoughts to stay in your mind, you are opening the door to trouble. Whatever you begin to dwell on is eventually what you will end up doing.

So please understand, every time you get afraid, it is not because an evil spirit jumped on you; it is due to you thinking contrary to the Word of God. This is why it is so important to stay in the Word. Keep your mind full of God thoughts! We cannot allow our thoughts to be on anything other than God. If our thoughts are on the circumstances, the fear will strengthen in our life and eventually take away your control.

CONTROLLED BY FEAR

Have you ever been around someone who is always scared or worried? These people are like a bunch of nut cases; every little thing freaks them out! I had a friend that always worried about something. This person worried about money, school, relationships, family, etc; you name it, they were afraid of it. They would ask my advice regarding a decision and as soon as I gave my answer, they would always counter with a possible negative situation as a result. This would go on and on until I was so frustrated, I had to simply walk away so I would not say something I would regret later!

I always look at my options from different angles (that is wisdom), but at some point, you must follow peace and make a decision. Colossians 3:15 says, *"And let the peace of God rule in your hearts"* and that is how I endeavor to live my life each and every day. Although, people living in and controlled by fear will never be able to follow peace, much less make a worthwhile decision. It will be a miracle if those types of people ever make a decision! *I have learned over the years that being worried or afraid never changes the situation; it only changes me.* Fear changes you; faith changes your situation!

PLAYING SKEERED

Growing up, I was very involved in sports, especially basketball. My sophomore year of high school, I made the varsity squad. We were in a very tough district and played some of the top teams in the state of Texas as well as two of the top players in the country; it was fairly easy to be intimidated.

I used to get so nervous before those district games that it usually took me until halftime just to get the jitters out of my head and my stomach. When I played scared, I looked it; someone with a melted heart is very noticeable!

I would miss shots because I shot timidly and would get the ball stolen because I was afraid someone would steal it. By halftime, I would be so mad at myself that I would go out and play without being scared - this is also the reason I always played bad in the first half and great in the second half. I learned one thing very quickly: never play scared, because if you play scared, you will lose!

It was not until my senior year that I began to take control of my mind before games. Coach Sebek used to tell me, "Stop playing skeered. If you are skeered, then you will play skeered!" (If you haven't figured out, Coach was a little country!) I became tired of his comments because I knew it was true; so, I made a change. I decided I was unstoppable and was no longer going to play scared.

When I went out with the attitude that I was unstoppable, I played that way. I developed to the point that it didn't matter who it was or how tall they were - I took it to them. As soon as I stepped onto the court, I was ready to punish somebody. I always wanted to guard the best player so I could embarrass and shut him down; I was ready to play anyone regardless of size or talent.

It really did not take long to develop this attitude. I soon realized the greater One was within me and nothing could stop me unless I allowed it. I began quoting "I can do all things through Christ Who strengthens me" before every game and before every free throw.

I remember one particular game in which we were down by one point with eleven seconds left. The team we were playing was a big rival and it was an important game because it had a deciding factor in playoff berths. We had drawn up an inbounds play and the pass came to me. I made a move, got open, took the shot and missed. Fortunately, I got my own rebound and was fouled.

There were six seconds left and the game's outcome was resting on me; I had two free throws to take and we needed both to win. Now I was averaging almost 90% from the free throw line, so I was pretty consistent, but at this point, I was extremely nervous. The pressure was high, the crowd was screaming, and I could feel the wishful prayers of my coach and teammates. I stepped up to the line and the referee gave me the ball. I then went through my routine…five dribbles, a spin of the ball, quoted Philippians 4:13…and shot the ball. It wasn't the prettiest free throw (my hands and fingers were so sweaty that the ball slipped a little), but it rattled around and went in. Our fans started screaming, the other team called a timeout, and I finally took a breath.

As I walked over to the bench, I knew why the opposing team called the timeout; they wanted me to think about that next free throw and their strategy was definitely working. I started thinking about the next free throw and continued to become more nervous. My coach pulled out his clipboard and I'll never forget his words: "After Chad hits this next free throw, this is what we are going to do…"

His words shook me and helped me refocus my thinking. I straightened up and got those stupid thoughts of failure, defeat, and fear out of my mind and began confessing, "I can do all things through Christ Who strengthens me; I will not be afraid!" I regained my composure and confidence and was ready to go.

The buzzer rang and it was time for the next free throw. I can honestly say that before I ever stepped to the line, I knew I was not going to miss. I was so confident, I actually looked to the crowd (it was our opponent's home gym) and conveyed that I was going to make it - which in turn sent some unbecoming compliments and gestures my way! The fans had really been riding me the whole game and this was my chance to shut them up for good.

Anyway, back to the spiritual part of this book…I took control of the fearful thoughts and began thinking God thoughts. I stepped to the line with everyone's eyes on me and six seconds left in the game; the score was 90-90. I got the ball, went through my routine and released the ball. It was smooth, beautiful, and nothing but net. Score: 90-91. Needless to say, we played good defense for the next few seconds and won the game. By confessing and dwelling on the Word, fear left, boldness took came, and I took control of my situation.

I hope now you understand that fear is a belief which is a result of your thoughts.   Remember, Jesus never cast out a spirit of fear. You will never find one instance in the Bible where a spirit of fear was cast out of anyone; yet, repeatedly in our churches, Sunday school lessons, books, television, internet, etc, we are told to cast out or rebuke the spirit of fear "In the Name of Jesus." Jesus never cast out a fearful spirit, but always commanded the disciples not to fear and has commanded us not to fear. Why are we told not to fear? Because we control our beliefs and it is our responsibility to maintain our thought life.

Chapter Seven

Continual Awareness

We must continually be aware and sensitive to the Presence of God in our lives. We have learned through this study that God is with us. He never leaves us nor forsakes us; therefore, we never have to be afraid. Yet, as with every truth in the Word of God, it is simply not enough to have knowledge of the truth; we must put the knowledge into practice in order to see results. We can believe that Jesus was the Son of God and that He provided salvation for us through His sacrifice; yet, possession of our salvation will not occur without the confession of that truth. *Knowledge without action is simply wasted information.* The truth by itself will not set you free; it is your acting on the truth that will set you free.

We can believe that God continually abides within us, but unless we begin to act on that truth, we will never see the effect of God's abiding presence in our lives. You may say, "Chad, how can I possibly act on the truth that God is in me?" Well, that's easy - simply act like He is there. Think and act the way you would if you could physically see Jesus at your side. Begin talking to Him; start spending time with Him.

You can have a conversation wherever you are. I wouldn't recommend you doing so around other people; they might think you are missing a few brain cells (adults don't take too kindly to other adults having invisible friends!) Anyways, take advantage of the opportunities you have. Spend time in the Word. Spend time praying in the Spirit. The more time we spend in the Word and in prayer, the more we meditate and talk about heavenly things, the more aware we will be of His continual, abiding presence.

God's presence should be more real to you than all those around you. You may say that is not possible, but it is true. You should desire to have the same awareness of God's presence as we see in Adam. Adam knew when God was there. He walked with Him and talked with Him; Adam daily fellowshipped with the God of the Universe. The opportunity is available for God to be more real to you than the clothes on your back.

Kenneth E. Hagin stated numerous times that God was more real to him than his wife of over 60 years. As I continue in my walk with the Lord, I am gradually finding that He is more real to me than those around me. This is being achieved because I am simply spending more time dwelling on His Word, His will, and His ways. The more I think about Him being with me, the more real He becomes; conversely, the less time I spend thinking about His abiding presence, the more my awareness of Him begins to fade.

When I first began studying along the lines of fear and God's abiding presence, I was spending vast amounts of time meditating on the truths that I have presented to you. About that time, someone broke into my home around 3:00am. When I got out of bed, a boldness rose up within me; I was conscious of God's presence with me!

Now mind you, I didn't have a gun, a baseball bat, or even a frying pan. It was just me, God and my 2 boxers, Buster and Lucy. I went all through that dim house opening up doors, looking in closets and checking under beds, until I found he had escaped through a window. I can honestly say through the whole ordeal that not once was I afraid. I was well aware that God was with me and my ministering angels were around me.   Let us contrast that to this next situation.

Approximately one month later, we had another break in. Now, in the preceding weeks, I had become very busy and my study time had been affected; I had not spent much time maintaining my awareness of His abiding presence. When the second break-in occurred, I was scared. I started fearfully confessing "God is with me, God is with me!" but I was still scared; I even had a baseball bat this time!

As I cautiously went through the house, I felt like it was just me and Buster…no God, no angels…just me, my bat and my dog! The confidence I had the first time was severely missing the second time and the cause was a lack of awareness of Who was within me.

As an added note, that night I took control of the situation. I went outside and walked the boundaries of my property. I boldly declared my property was covered by the Blood of Jesus and Satan was not to come on it again. I took authority and we have never had a problem since that time.

As I spend greater amounts of time praying in the Spirit, the more real He becomes. As I continually live my life as if He is physically right beside me, the more aware I become that He is closer than beside me - HE IS IN ME! Praise God! As we increasingly spend time talking and thinking about heavenly things, we will find that our awareness of heavenly things will increase as well. Let the reality of God's abiding presence continue to become increasingly real in your life.

So, in summary, what have we learned?

1. *Fear will melt your heart.*
2. *Melted hearts destroy your hope, your courage and your strength.*
3. *Fear is not a spirit, but a belief.*
4. *Fear is the result of abandoning our knowledge of God's abiding presence.*
5. *If you do not want fearful thoughts, think on God's Word.*
6. *If you want Bible results, you must follow Bible directions.*
7. *You were designed to be fearless, for you are more than a conqueror and the Spirit of God dwells in you.*
8. *The answer for fear? God is here!*

Closing

The choice is now yours. You have been given the information and presented with the truth, yet what you do with it is entirely up to you. As I told you previously, knowledge without action is wasted information. You can be full of life changing truths, but unless you act on them, you and the rest of the world will never see your life changed. The doers of the Word are those who are blessed, so I challenge you to be a doer of the truths presented.

Fearful or fearless...what do you choose?

Prayer for Salvation and Baptism of the Holy Spirit

It is the desire of God that everyone accept His free gift of salvation. God sent the greatest gift Heaven had so the world could be set free; that precious gift was Jesus! Despite knowing the sins you would commit, He died for you anyway. Why? His love was greater than your sin.

Romans 10:9-10 says if you will confess Jesus as your Lord and Savior and believe that He rose from the dead, you will be saved. You see, salvation has nothing to do with works (Ephesians 2:8-9). It doesn't matter what church you belong to, how many little old ladies you help across the street or how much you give toward the church. You can not earn salvation, you can not buy salvation; you must simply accept salvation.

Another free gift God has provided is the baptism of the Holy Spirit. In Acts 2, we find the gift of the Holy Spirit being given to the Church. God desires that you be filled with His Spirit with the evidence of speaking in tongues. God said in Acts 2:38 that this life changing gift was for everyone, not just a select few. It was not set aside for just the 12 disciples or the early Church; it was given for all who would accept His precious Son Jesus! The infilling of the Holy Spirit will allow you operate in the fullness of God's power and be a blessing to the entire world.

If you have never accepted Jesus as your Lord and Savior or accepted

God's gift of being filled with the Holy Spirit, I invite you to pray the following prayer:

Father, I believe that you sent Jesus to the earth just for me. I believe that He died on the cross and arose from the dead. I confess Him as my Savior and accept Him as Lord over my life. I thank you that by His sacrifice, my sins have been forgiven and I am a new creature in Christ Jesus! I am now your child!

I now ask you for the infilling of the Holy Spirit with the evidence of speaking in tongues. You said in Your Word it was a gift, so I ask you for it and receive it right now. I thank you for my heavenly language.

Thank you for your mercy! Thank you for being in love with me! Thank you for being my Father! Thank you for your goodness!

We encourage you to become involved in a solid, Bible-based church. Begin praying in the Spirit daily and spend time reading your Bible. Now it is time to start growing in the Lord…and don't forget to tell somebody about what Jesus did for you! Remember, God is exceedingly, abundantly good!

If you prayed this prayer, or this book has impacted your life in any way, we would love to hear from you! Visit us on our website, send us a note and check out all of our other books and teaching resources.

www.ChadGonzales.com

Study Guide

Chapter One - Melted Hearts

1. What does it mean when the Bible states that fear caused people's hearts to melt?

_____

_____

2. What were the four examples of "melted hearts" given in the chapter?

_____

_____

_____

3. Why were the people of Jericho afraid and according to Rahab, "lost their courage to fight?"

_____

_____

4. What are the seven reasons fear must be not be allowed to operate in our lives?

_____

_____

_____

_____

5. What did you learn most from Chapter One?

_____

_____

DISCUSSION

Talk about a situation in your life when you allowed fear to "melt your heart." How did you react to the situation? How should you have responded to the situation?

Chapter Two - The Result of Knowledge

1. Hosea 4:6 says that God's people are destroyed because of a lack of _____.

2. _____ is the result of knowledge.

3. When you know what God's Word says about your situation, it automatically causes faith to rise up. What happens when you don't know what God's Word says about your situation?

_____

_____

DISCUSSION

Think back to a time when you were scared. What were the circumstances that caused the fear? How would you react now in the same situation?

Chapter Three - The Answer For Fear

1. What was the source of David's confidence that he could kill Goliath? _____

2. In Psalm 46:1, we are told that God is a _____ help in a time of trouble.

3. Fear will cause you to run away from your enemies. Faith will cause you to do what? _____

4. The answer for fear is _____.

5. List the twelve scriptures that prove the answer for fear.

_____

_____

_____

_____

_____

_____

DISCUSSION

When children are scared, they always cry out for their parents because their parent's presence brings confidence. How does this compare with our relationship with our Heavenly Father?

Chapter Four - The Identity of Fear

1. 2 Timothy 1:7 says _____

_____ .

2. Explain 2 Timothy 1:7. _____

_____

3. Why is fear not a spirit? _____

_____

_____

4. When Jesus was dealing with fearful people, how did He respond?

_____

_____

5. Name a person and the scripture reference in which Jesus dealt with them regarding fear. _____

_____

DISCUSSION

Why do you think people refer to fear as being a spirit?

Chapter Five - Knock, Knock

1. What does Romans 10:17 say? _____

_____

2. What are the two doors through which fear enters? _____

_____

3. What you believe is determined by what you _____?

4. How can we feed our faith and starve our fears?

_____

_____

_____

5. You are what you _____?

DISCUSSION

What are some ways that you have fed your fears in the past? Are these things you are still doing? If so, what do you need to change?

Chapter Six - Mind Control

1. What are God's instructions found in Philippians 4:6-8?

_____

_____

_____

2. Why does Satan bring thoughts of fear and doubt?

_____

_____

3. If you had peace about a situation and that peace is now gone, it probably means you have _____ .

4. What does the Amplified version of Colossians 3:15 say?

_____

_____

5. When Jesus was in the Garden of Gethsamene, He was obviously dealing with stress and fear. How did He deal with it?

_____

_____

DISCUSSION

Talk about why Jesus doesn't have authority over your thought life.

Chapter Seven - Continual Awareness

1. Knowledge without action is simply _____.

2. God's presence should be more real to you than _____
_____.

3. Why is it important to have a continual awareness of God?

_____

_____

DISCUSSION

How can you maintain an awarenes of God's presence in your life?